MAR 0 2 '10	DATE DUE		
APR 0 1 '11			

COSTUME, TRADITION, AND CULTURE:
REFLECTING ON THE PAST

Ancient Warriors

by

Dwayne E. Pickels

Chelsea House Publishers
Philadelphia

CHELSEA HOUSE PUBLISHERS

Editor-in-Chief Stephen Reginald
Managing Editor James D. Gallagher
Production Manager Pamela Loos
Art Director Sara Davis
Picture Editor Judy Hasday
Senior Production Editor Lisa Chippendale
Designer Takeshi Takahashi

First Printing

1 3 5 7 9 8 6 4 2

Library of Congress Cataloging-in-Publication Data

Pickels, Dwayne E.
Ancient warriors / by Dwayne E. Pickels.

    p. cm. — (Costume, tradition, and culture: reflecting on
the past)
Includes bibliographical references and index.
Summary: Provides an overview of the military exploits of
twenty-five nations, tribes, or peoples from history, including
the Angles, Huns, Magyars, Romans, Samurai, and Vikings.

ISBN 0–7910–5166–8 (hardcover)
1. Military history, Ancient—Juvenile literature. 2. Civilization, Ancient—Juvenile literature. [1. Military history.]
I. Title. II. Series.
D25.5.P53 1998
930'.03—dc21
                                          98-29900
                                          CIP
                                          AC

CONTENTS

INTRODUCTION

For as long as people have known that other cultures existed, they have been curious about the differences in their customs and traditions. Julius Caesar, the famous Roman leader, wrote long chronicles about the inhabitants of Gaul (modern-day France) while he was leading troops in the Gallic Wars (58–51 B.C.). In the chronicles, he discussed their religious beliefs, their customs, their day-to-day life, and the conflicts among the different groups. Explorers like Marco Polo traveled thousands of miles and devoted years of their lives to learning about the peoples of the East and bringing home the stories of Chinese court life, along with the silks, spices, and inventions of that culture. The Chelsea House series *Costume, Tradition, and Culture: Reflecting on the Past* continues this legacy of exploration and discovery by discussing some of the most fascinating traditions, beliefs, legends, and artifacts from around the world.

Different cultures develop traditions and costumes to mark the roles of people in their societies, to commemorate events in their histories, and to make the changes and mysteries of life more meaningful. Soldiers wear uniforms to show that they are serving in their nation's army, and insignia on the uniforms show what ranks they hold within the army. People of Bukhara, a city in Uzbekistan, have for centuries woven fine threads of gold into their clothes, and when they travel to other cities they can be recognized as Bukharans by the golden embroidery on their traditional costume. For many years, in the Irish countryside, people would leave bowls of milk outside at night as an offering to the fairies, or "Good People," believing that this would help ensure their favor and keep the family safe from fairy mischief. In Mexico, November 2 is the Day of the Dead, when people visit cemeteries and have feasts to remember their ancestors. In the United States, brides wear white dresses, and the traditional wedding includes many rituals: the father of the bride "giving her away" to the groom, the exchange of vows and rings, the throwing of rice, the tossing of the bride's bouquet. These rituals and symbols help make the marriage meaningful and special for the couple, their families, and their friends, by expressing the change that is taking place and allowing the friends and families to wish luck to the couple.

This series will explore some of the myths, symbols, costumes, and traditions of various cultures from around the world and different times in the past. *Fighting Units of the American War of Independence,* for example, will detail the uniforms, weapons, and decorations of the regiments and battalions on both sides of the war, along with the battles in which they became famous. *Roman Myths, Heroes, and Legends* describes how the ancient Romans explained the wonders and natural phenomena of their world with fantastic stories of superhuman heroes and almost human deities who could change the course of history at will. In *Popular Superstitions,* you will learn how some familiar superstitious beliefs—such as throwing spilled salt over your shoulder, or hanging a horseshoe over your door for good luck—originally began, in times when people feared that devils and evil spirits were meddling in their lives. Few people still believe in malicious spirits, but many still toss the spilled salt over their shoulders, or knock on wood when expressing cautious hope. The legendary figures of a culture—the brave explorers of *The Wild West* or the wicked brigands described in *Infamous Pirates*— help shape that culture's values by providing grand, almost mythical examples of what people should (or should not!) strive to be.

The illustrations that accompany these books have their own cultural history. Originally, they were printed on small collectors' cards and sold in the early 20th century. Each card in a set of 25 or 50 would depict a different person, artifact, or event, and usually the reverse side would offer a few sentences of description to explain the picture. Now, they provide a fascinating glimpse into history and an entertaining addition to the stories presented here.

ABOUT THE AUTHOR

DWAYNE E. PICKELS is an award-winning reporter with the *Greensburg (PA) Tribune-Review.* A magna cum laude graduate of the University of Pittsburgh, where he cofounded and edited the literary magazine *Pendulum,* Dwayne won a Pennsylvania Newspaper Publishers' Association (PNPA) Keystone Press Award in 1992. The author of a number of books for Chelsea House, Dwayne lives in Scottdale, Pennsylvania, with his wife, Mary, and their daughter, Kaidia Leigh. In his free time, he is immersed in a number of literary pursuits—which include a novel based on Celtic myth and legend. In addition to writing, Dwayne enjoys outdoor excursions, including bird watching, hiking, photography, and target shooting, along with typically futile attempts at fishing.

OVERVIEW

Ancient Warriors

Through hundreds and thousands of years, wars of all kinds have been fought on scales large and small, for reasons large and small. Nations have fought to protect their homeland or to destroy the homeland of the "enemy," to advance their own religion or to deny someone else's. There was even a war fought a few years ago in Central America over a soccer game.

And whether we like it or not, the warrior—the person who devotes his life to war and fighting—has been part of civilization since humans arose. As civilization evolved, warriors were necessary members of society; they both advanced and protected their community's rights and property.

A warrior fought with whatever was available—whether bare hands or simple materials such as fire or stones. Missiles and launchers—slings, spears, and arrows—joined common agricultural and hand tools like hammers and axes on the early battlefield. Technological advances led to bronze and later steel blades and armor that could be used by soldiers on horseback and in war chariots. Later, the invention of gunpowder changed the warfare forever, leading eventually to rapid-fire, incendiary, and explosive weapons. In the 20th century, the 1940s saw the development of the most fearful weapon used to date—the atomic bomb.

Weapons technology and military tactics are still evolving, and the direction warfare will next take is as fascinating to some as it is terrifying to others. Yet whether looked at with fear or with excitement, warfare must be looked at, for only through accurate knowledge of the world can we come to deal with its overwhelming issues. And central to our understanding of warfare is the soul of the warrior, which has fired and haunted humankind.

Ancient Greeks

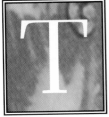 he Greeks, one of the first European civilizations, inhabited the land that is now known as Greece and also part of Asia Minor. Ancient Greece was ruled by a system of city-states, representing a variety of ethnic groups, which sometimes formed alliances to fight against each other and against common foes. The Greeks' principal enemies were the Persians, with whom they continually warred.

The two most prominent city-states were Athens and Sparta. The Athenians could prove to be formidable opponents when provoked. Primarily, though, Athens was known for its thinkers, artists, and philosophers. Sparta was the city-state most famous for its warrior class. No one doubted the Spartans' prowess on the battlefield.

Greek soldiers are said to have fought ferociously. Although they relied primarily on infantry—some of them clad in ornate bronze armor—the ancient Greeks also developed a strong navy.

Two of Greece's greatest leaders—the Macedonian warrior-king Philip II and his better-known son, Alexander the Great—welded the Greek race into one empire in the fourth century B.C., and they greatly expanded the kingdom through a 10-year surge of invasion and conquest.

The art, philosophy, and other more peaceful contributions of Greek culture live on in modern times. But with Alexander's death, Greece's military empire disintegrated. Ultimately the Greeks were conquered and engulfed by the next great military machine to arise in the Mediterranean region—the Romans.

ANGLES

The Angles were a Teutonic race, and it is from this German tribe that the name of England—Angleland—derives.

The Angles originally came from the Angul region of the Jutland Peninsula, located to the south of modern Denmark. The term *anglers,* used to describe fishermen, is said to come from the distinctive shape of this land mass, which resembles a fishhook.

In the fifth century the Angles began raids on England. These raids—along with those of the Saxons and the Jutes—followed the Romans' departure from the British Isles. Soon the various Germanic groups established kingdoms in England. The Angles settled in the countryside, especially in the eastern region known as East Anglia, and intermarried with the native Celtic people, beginning the Anglo-Celtic civilization. Some of the Angle tribes became so intermixed with neighboring Saxons that they later became known as the Anglo-Saxons.

This new hybrid race faced a formidable challenge in A.D. 1066, when Duke William of Normandy brought his Norman hordes across the English Channel to wrest the English throne from King Harold II. The Normans were descendants of Viking raiders who had settled in northern France, in the region still known as Normandy. Though fierce and courageous, the troops of the Anglo-Saxons and other tribes who fought to defend England were primarily a peasant militia. They fell easily to William's forces, which included mail-clad cavalry supported by archers and heavily armored infantry. The Norman duke was crowned king of the English on Christmas Day, 1066.

ASSYRIANS

The he Assyrians lived on the northern Tigris River, in the part of the Middle East that the ancient Greeks called Mesopotamia.

The Assyrian territory began small, featuring only three cities in the period from 1800 to 1600 B.C. But beginning in the ninth century B.C., the Assyrians expanded their kingdom into an empire by conquering neighboring peoples, including the Hittites and Babylonians. At its height around 650 B.C., the Assyrian Empire reached from the eastern shores of the Mediterranean Sea to the northwestern banks of the Persian Gulf. It boasted the major cities of Jerusalem, Tyre, Sidon, and Babylon, as well as the Assyrians' own capital, Nineveh.

Soon after, though, the Assyrian realm fell apart. In 612 B.C. Nineveh fell to the Babylonians, who had allied with the Medes. With amazing rapidity the Assyrians disappeared from history.

The Assyrians are said to have worn great beards and ringleted hair, tall hats, and long robes. Adopting cavalry forces and three-man war chariots, the Assyrians developed their military art to a high degree. However, their primary force was their infantry, which fought with pikes, bows and arrows, and short swords. The Assyrians also had units of heavy infantry equipped with protective armor. They used battering rams and siege towers to smash and penetrate fortifications.

Despite their military prowess, the Assyrians suffered from political unrest and internal struggles for power, which played a major role in the empire's downfall.

AZTECS

The Aztecs were the original inhabitants of the southern regions of North America, known today as Mexico. According to one of their legends, they would build their great kingdom on a swampy site where they would see an eagle eating a snake while perched on a cactus growing out of a rock. Aztec priests reportedly saw this sign when they arrived—along with waves of other immigrant tribes—in the western region of the central plateau area around Lake Texcoco. This occurred after the decline of the Toltec civilization in the 11th century.

The Aztecs rose to dominance with advanced military and social structures. They founded the city of Tenochtitlán on the site of present-day Mexico City in 1325. Their empire stretched from central Mexico to Guatemala when it was invaded by Hernando Cortez and his Spanish forces in 1519.

At first, the Aztecs were victorious over the Spanish invaders, surrounding Cortez's forces and capturing his guns and horses. However, the ruthless Spaniard escaped and later returned to exact a horrible vengeance. The Aztecs were vanquished and the entire country subjugated under Spanish rule.

Before their struggles with the Europeans, the Aztecs had developed elaborate writing, mathematical, and astronomical systems. They also erected fabulous stone monuments and temples, which included pyramids. Rituals associated with these structures included animal and even human sacrifices—an integral part of the Aztec religion. Aztec warriors are said to have considered it as great an honor to be sacrificed to one of their gods as to die in battle.

BABYLONIANS

The Babylonians inhabited the region of Asia Minor located between the Tigris and the Euphrates Rivers in the second and first millennia B.C. Their capital city was Babylon, located near the site of Baghdad in modern-day Iraq. Because of its position on a popular overland trade route between the Persian Gulf and the Mediterranean Sea, Babylon was one of the most important cities of the ancient world.

The people of that region were originally Sumerian tribes that united with the Semites under Sargon around 2330 B.C. Later they were subjected to invasions by warlike tribes that included the Amorites, with whom they subsequently united. The resultant people, the Babylonians, waged nearly perpetual war with Egyptians and Assyrians, eventually conquering the whole of Mesopotamia.

After its first flourishing, the Babylonian empire gradually declined, and control passed to the Assyrians in the eighth century B.C. However, a ruler named Nabopolassar once again drove out the Assyrians between 625 and 615 B.C. His successor, Nebuchadnezzar II, continued to revive the fortunes of Babylon and raised the empire to its greatest heights of power and glory, encompassing much of southwest Asia.

The nation eventually fell to Cyrus the Great, a Persian ruler, in 539 B.C. Two centuries later, the Macedonian general Alexander the Great conquered the city of Babylon.

CARTHAGINIANS

The Carthaginians were inhabitants of ancient Carthage in North Africa, which was established by the Phoenicians in 814 B.C. The Carthaginians were renowned sailors as well as warriors. Despite a preference for using mercenaries rather than spilling the blood of their own people, the Carthaginians' influence was felt up and down the Mediterranean. Thus they came under the jealous eye of Rome.

In the First Punic War, from 264 to 241 B.C., the Romans defeated the Carthaginians in several sea battles—primarily because the traditionally nonseafaring Romans adopted military strategies like "boarding planks" that turned maritime combat into infantry conflicts.

It was during the Second Punic War, from 218 to 201 B.C., that history's most celebrated Carthaginian leader, Hannibal, arose. Hannibal led his men—some atop elephants—over the Alps and into Italy to harass the Roman forces for about 15 years. However, he was forced to return to Carthage when his supplies were cut off and his brother, Hasdrubal, suffered the loss of an entire army. At the battle of Zama in 202 B.C., Hannibal experienced his first crushing defeat, and Carthage sued for peace. This time, the Carthaginians were stripped of all their possessions and wealth and forced to abandon their territories in Spain.

During the Third Punic War, from 149 to 146 B.C., the Romans took Carthage itself and literally poured salt over the ruins of the city. They forbade anyone to occupy the site for a quarter of a century.

CHINESE

Dating back some 3,500 years, the Chinese civilization is considered the oldest in the world. The Chinese are said to have been a cultured people while the rest of the world was still struggling through barbarianism.

A Chinese thinker, Sun Tzu, published the first known treatise on combat, *The Art of War,* around 400 B.C. At some point before A.D. 1000, the Chinese produced the first gunpowder weapons, which forever changed the course of world conflict. They also developed superior naval and navigational skills, and with these advanced scientific and military technologies they founded great and powerful dynasties.

As a result, most of the battles fought by Chinese warriors were against their fellow countrymen, in political struggles between rival clans and dynasties. Nevertheless, between 220 and 205 B.C., the Chinese created a protective wall of earth, stone, and brick to defend the country's northern borders from nomadic tribes. This barrier became known as the Great Wall of China. It was extended in the fourth century A.D. and again under the Ming Dynasty, a thousand years later. Eventually it stretched some 1,500 miles and stood an average of 25 feet tall.

With the help of the wall, the Chinese were able to keep out most hordes of barbarians. By the end of the 13th century A.D., however, ferocious Mongol warriors, led by Genghis Khan and then by his grandson, Kublai Khan, laid claim to all of China. In 1368 a Chinese revolt once again restored China's independence, establishing the famous Ming Dynasty that lasted nearly 300 years.

DANES

The Danes were so-called Northmen from Scandinavia, one of the Nordic peoples who became known as Vikings. In the Vikings' heyday, from the 9th to the 11th centuries A.D., they raided and invaded many parts of Europe.

From their main base in the land that became Denmark, the Danes made daring seafaring raids into France, the Netherlands, Spain, and Italy. Principally, though, they invaded England and fought with the Saxons. They conquered and settled in the north and east of England, but were constantly warring with the Saxons in the south.

Their greatest leader, Canute, became king of England in A.D. 1016 and soon added Denmark and Norway to his realm. However, the Danish influence in England did not last beyond his death. Eventually the Saxons and the Danes united.

The Danes also made eastward expansions in the late 12th and early 13th centuries, conquering large portions of the Baltic Sea coastal areas. In 1380 Denmark joined with Norway under King Olaf II. That union also included Iceland, Greenland, and the Faroe Islands. In 1389, under the rule of Olaf's mother, Margaret I, the crown of Sweden was added to the alliance. This led in 1397 to what was known as the Kalmar Union, an unsteady partnership with Denmark at the center of power, that lasted until Sweden and Finland revolted against the Danish king in 1523.

Similar struggles continued through subsequent centuries. The present-day country of Denmark consists of most of the Jutland Peninsula and about 500 islands, of which fewer than 200 are inhabited.

FRANKS

he Teutonic tribes that came to be known as the Franks emerged from the middle and lower regions of the Rhine River in the middle of the third century A.D. The Frankish groups included the Salians, the Ripuarians, and the Chatti, all of whom spoke the same language. Around A.D. 250 they began to wander into Roman provinces.

In the fifth century, with the decline of the Roman Empire, Frankish territories spread westward to the Atlantic Ocean, engulfing the region then known as Gaul (now France). New recruits from Germany continually reinforced this advance guard of Germans as they pressed toward the west. Frankish warriors are said to have been great fighters who dominated Gaul through sheer perseverance.

One famous Frankish leader was Clovis I, a Salian Frank who became king in 481 and overthrew the last Roman ruler in Gaul in 486. Ten years later, Clovis was converted to Christianity and launched what became a continuing bond between the Frankish government and the Roman Catholic Church.

With Clovis's death, the Frankish kingdom, which then stretched from the Pyrenees Mountains to Friesland, was divided among his four sons. Later it expanded into Saxon-held territories under the auspices of such rulers as Charles Martel, Pepin the Short, and Charlemagne. In the mid-ninth century the Frankish lands were split once again, creating a West Frankish kingdom that became France and an East Frankish kingdom that became Germany.

GOTHS

The Goths, another Teutonic people, apparently migrated across the Baltic Sea from Sweden. In the third century A.D. they crossed the Danube River and came up against the might of Rome. Wars between Goths and Romans decimated the northeast Mediterranean region and the Balkans for about 100 years before the Goths established a kingdom that stretched from the Baltic Sea to the Black Sea. Then, in the fourth century, the Goths split into two distinct groups—the Visigoths and the Ostrogoths.

The Visigoths, or western Goths, sought Roman protection from the Huns in 376 and were granted a haven to the south of the Danube River. However, the Visigoths revolted against their Roman guardians, threatening the new Roman capital of Constantinople before they once again joined the Roman legions. They became the first Germanic tribe to become Christianized.

In 395, they again renounced Roman allegiance and invaded Greece and Italy, sacking Rome in 410 under King Alaric. They then crossed the Pyrenees Mountains to invade Spain and southern Gaul (France). In later centuries, their power declined in conflicts with the Franks and the Moors.

Meanwhile, the Ostrogoths were overrun in 370 by the Huns and many were assimilated into their culture. Most of those who joined the campaigns of the Huns' leader, Attila, were slain by Visigoths when the Huns invaded Gaul in 451. Theodoric, king of an Ostrogoth faction that had sought sanctuary with the Romans, became the first Gothic ruler of the western Roman Empire in A.D. 493. However, the rise of the Byzantine Empire devastated Gothic power, and the Goths were gradually absorbed by tribes such as the Vandals and the Franks.

HUNS

The Huns were a nomadic Asian people who thundered across the Caspian steppes of present-day southern Russia to harry the Roman legions during the fourth and fifth centuries A.D. They were most likely descended from the Turks or Tartars of Mongolia in central Asia.

The Huns were renowned for their cruelty and destructiveness, massacring local inhabitants and turning the fertile lands they conquered to desert. One of the Hun warrior's greatest attributes was his prowess in cavalry warfare; the Huns were regarded as expert equestrians. However, the various peoples they crushed were typically assimilated into the conquerors' culture, altering the ethnic and social character of the horde, so that the Huns ultimately lost their separate identity.

At the height of their rise, the Huns divided into two tribes—one invaded and ravaged China; the other went westward, wandered over Europe, and settled in Hungary.

The western Huns became the principal foes of Rome and Byzantium—the capitals of the eastern and western realms of the Roman Empire, which they nearly brought to its knees. Under their most famous leader, Attila, the Huns delivered several paralyzing blows to both halves of the empire in the fifth century. Later, the Hun warriors joined forces with the Visigoths, their former foes, to invade Gaul and northern Italy.

With the death of Attila in 453, the Huns' power declined and their warriors were absorbed by the surrounding populations. Many enrolled in the Roman legions; others offered their services to new hordes of invaders attacking the empire from the north and the east.

INCAS

The Incas were originally inhabitants of the Andes Mountains in Peru, South America. By the time of the arrival of Spaniards in the Western Hemisphere, they ruled an empire that stretched more than 2,000 miles in length, through mountains, rain forests, and deserts. Little is known about Inca origins, because legend merged with fact in the histories passed down through their Spanish conquerors.

Most of this empire was acquired in a few decades of the 15th century through often vicious warfare with other tribes. The Incas fought mostly hand-to-hand, being unfamiliar with either firearms or wheeled vehicles. Travel was on foot or by llamas (which were more often used as pack animals).

Regarded as fierce, brutal warriors, they were nonetheless a cultured race with a high level of civilization. Their agricultural skill included complicated hillside terracing and irrigation systems. They were also superb builders, constructing rope suspension bridges, massive stone temples, and stone steps carved into mountainsides. Their system of 20,000 kilometers (12,000 miles) of roads was surpassed only by the Romans in the ancient world. The roads aided both in rapid conquest and in administration.

A sun-worshipping people, the Incas mined gold, a symbol of the sun, to decorate their temples. In 1532, Spanish explorer Francisco Pizarro invaded Peru with a force of less than 200 men armed with firearms. Pizarro took the emperor, Atahualpa, hostage with the help of Atahualpa's enemies and demanded an enormous sum of gold as ransom. The ransom was paid, but the Spaniards killed the emperor. Without leadership, the Incas' political organization quickly dissolved, leaving South America open to Spanish expansion.

ISRAELITES

he Israelites were a race of 12 tribes of Jewish warriors whose kingdom once included the region of present-day Israel, parts of Jordan, and the southern regions of Syria in southwest Asia. The Jews' exodus from Egypt and subsequent years of wandering through the wilderness prior to their invasion of the Holy Land—Canaan (later known as Palestine)—are well documented, thanks to the Bible.

Israel is thought to have emerged as a nation in the 11th century B.C., under the rule of King Saul. His successor, Kind David, expanded the empire to include what is now Lebanon, Syria, Jordan, and Egypt.

David's son, Solomon, launched a massive building campaign that produced many fabulous temples and royal palaces in Israel's capital city, Jerusalem. But Solomon's reportedly oppressive rule helped foster the dissension that led to a subsequent division of the kingdom.

Following Solomon's death around 922 B.C., the kingdom of Israel was divided into two parts—Israel proper, to the north, and Judah, to the south. The northern realm was sacked by the Assyrians in 722 B.C. Judah held out until about the sixth century B.C. before being conquered by the Babylonians.

All of Palestine later fell to the conquests of Alexander the Great and then to the Egyptians and the Syrians. An independent Jewish state that resurfaced in the second century B.C. was engulfed by the Romans, who dispersed the Jews once again, following the brutal destruction of Jerusalem in A.D. 70 and an insurrection in the second century A.D. Control of the territory latter went to the Byzantine Empire, only to be lost to Islamic Arabs in A.D. 630.

JUTES

The Jutes are perhaps the most aptly named of the Teutonic tribes that hailed from Jutland—the present-day peninsula of Denmark situated between the North and Baltic seas. Along with the Angles and the Saxons, the Jutes invaded the region of England known as Kent in the fifth century A.D. Their migration came in the wake of Roman withdrawal from the British Isles, at a time when other Germanic tribes were invading and sacking Rome.

After skirmishing with the native Celtic inhabitants and driving them westward to what is now Wales, the Jutes settled in that part of the county, and also on the Isle of Wight. They later blended with the Angles and Saxons to become the Anglo-Saxons, who became further blended in the wake of the Norman invasion led by William the Conqueror in 1066. The Norman warriors were descendants of Vikings who had settled in France.

Under the Anglo-Saxon warrior system, each leader or "eorl" could demand military service from his followers or "thanes"—roughly what we think of as knights, though before the days of massive armor. In turn, the lord guaranteed to protect the thanes' land.

The best-known leaders of the Jutes were Hengest and Horsa, brothers who led a Jutish invasion in A.D. 449. The history written by St. Bede the Venerable indicates the siblings were invited by the inhabitants to settle on the Isle of Thanet to drive away the dreaded warrior Picts who were pressing into the country from the north.

The Jutes defeated the Picts and settled in the area of Aylesford, Kent. However, by the eighth century, the term Jute had all but disappeared from the English language.

MAGYARS

he Magyars were a nomadic warrior tribe originating (3000 B.C. to A.D. 500) in northeastern Europe around the Volga and Kama rivers. They were related to the Huns and Turks and like them fought on horseback. Along their travels, there is some record of their having settled on the north shore of the Black Sea just after A.D. 500.

In the seventh century, they began a westward migration from the Ural Mountains in the western region of present-day Russia—the traditional boundary between Asia and Europe.

The Magyars—or "Hungari," as Latin writers termed them—were the third Turanian race to occupy the area now known as Hungary. They arrived between 889 and 896 under the leadership of Arpad and Kukszan. They fought their way over the Carpathian Mountains in present-day Romania from the north, settling between the rivers Tisza and Danube. The 900-mile Carpathian range is an extension of the Alps.

The Magyars went on to conquer the kingdom of Moravia in the central region of Czechoslovakia, west of the Carpathians.

The nomadic warriors then pressed into Germany before being halted in 955 by Otto I, the king of Saxony, also known as Otto the Great. Otto also defeated the Poles and the Bohemians during this period, and he became the first man crowned emperor of the Holy Roman Empire, in 962, for aiding Pope John XII in a struggle with an Italian king.

The Magyars became Christians in the 11th century under King Stephen I and settled down to build the Hungarian state.

OTTOMAN TURKS

he Ottoman Turks, who built one of the most powerful empires in history, sprang from a splinter group of Turks who fled invading Tartars (Mongols) in western Turkestan. They wandered central Asia's hills, deserts, and mountains, and embraced Muslim religion and culture. They often served as mercenaries for the more organized Seljuk Turks. In the 13th century they found a haven in Asia Minor, under the leadership of Osman I, who founded the Ottoman Dynasty.

Gradually, the Ottoman Turks became an important force in the Middle East, and then the dominant people. They eventually pushed their way into Europe, making inroads on the Byzantine Empire. With the success of their raids into Christian territories, the Ottomans' empire expanded—stretching from the Danube River to the Euphrates River—and gradually surrounded the remnants of the shrunken Byzantine Empire.

Under Sultan Mehmed II, Ottoman Turks attacked and looted the Byzantine capital of Constantinople (present-day Istanbul) in 1453 and made it their own capital. The Ottomans' continued their campaigns in the 16th century under Selim I, nicknamed "the Terrible," and Suleiman I, "the Magnificent," who together conquered Syria, Palestine, Egypt, Arabia, Iraq, and Albania.

This period proved the Ottomans' pinnacle of conquest. A slow decline followed, arising from internal political corruption and military defeats at the hands of Austria, Russia, and Poland in the 17th and 18th centuries. The Ottomans continued to lose territories until World War I, when they sided with the losing Germans. At the end of the war in 1918, the empire was dissolved.

PERSIANS

The Persians were an Aryan tribe with a mixture of Mongolian blood. They migrated from central Asia into Persia—a high plateau in what is now Iran—around 1500 B.C. They were dominated by the Medes until 558 B.C., when Cyrus the Great overthrew the Medes and engulfed the Lydian and Babylonian kingdoms to establish the Persian Empire.

The realm was extended in 525 B.C. with the conquest of the Egyptians. Following a revolt by Greeks living under Persian rule, Darius the Great launched a campaign of vengeance in 493 B.C. against the European Greeks who had supported the rebels. This began a period of long and continuous wars between the Persians and the Greeks.

In a series of battles between 334 and 331 B.C., Alexander the Great, who began as king of Macedonia, north of Greece, defeated the Persians and added their empire to his kingdoms. Alexander amassed his empire during a stunning 10-year campaign of conquest, which began when he was in his early 20s.

Persian men were enlisted into Alexander's armies, and Persian women were integrated through marriage to his officers. After a brief resurgence following Alexander's death in 323 B.C., Persian generals engaged in a struggle for power. Seleucus I merged victorious and led the Persians to conquer Babylon once again in 312 B.C. and re-extended the empire.

After centuries of subordination to the Parthian Empire, the Persians fought the Romans, and, later still, the Byzantines. Eventually, they were invaded by the Arabs in the seventh century A.D. and converted to Islam.

PHOENICIANS

The Phoenicians were the inhabitants of a thin strip of land—some 200 miles in length and 5 to 15 miles wide—on the eastern coast of the Mediterranean Sea. Present-day Lebanon includes most of ancient Phoenicia.

Related to the Canaanites of ancient Palestine, the Phoenicians developed powerful city-states, including Tyre and Sidon. Egypt invaded and ruled Phoenicia from 1800 to 1400 B.C., when Hittite raids gave the Phoenicians a window of opportunity to revolt against their weakened oppressors. They won their independence, which lasted for about 350 years.

The Phoenicians were better known as traders and sailors than as warriors. Cedar wood from Phoenicia was imported into Egypt as early as 2000 B.C. At their height, Phoenician ships sailed the whole of the Mediterranean Sea, as well as the eastern and western coasts of Africa, dealing in dyes, wine, weapons, and ivory.

Other countries in the Mediterranean hired Phoenician ships for their own navies. The seafaring Phoenicians also founded numerous colonies, including Carthage in North Africa, which fought a series of early wars with Rome.

In the ninth century B.C., Phoenicia was conquered by the Assyrians. It fell under the Persian rule in 539 B.C. The Persian Empire, in turn, was taken by Alexander the Great around 333 B.C. The Phoenician people were gradually assimilated into the Greco-Macedonian civilization and lost their separate identity. Even the name Phoenicia vanished when the Romans took the territory and made it part of their province of Syria in 64 B.C.

ROMANS

The Romans were peerless conquerors who established the largest, most powerful empire of the ancient world, absorbing that of the ancient Greeks in the process. The warriors of that empire, the infamous Roman legions, were a source of envy as much as fear and despair among Rome's many enemies.

Rome was founded in 753 B.C. The city's first makeshift militias—probably armed with as many slingshots as swords—were overrun by invading Gauls, who sacked Rome in 390 B.C. This defeat prompted a restructuring of the legions, which were honed with vigorous training said to have been as intense as actual war. Discipline was also strictly ingrained into the legions, to the point that soldiers who showed cowardice in battle or fell asleep on sentry duty could be stoned or clubbed to death by their own comrades in arms.

Such pride and discipline were an essential part of the armies' success in battle. Each legion comprised 5,000 men. Some units were armed with bows, arrows, and javelins that served as long-range artillery to soften opposing forces. Foot soldiers were equipped with short stabbing swords and large rectangular shields that formed moving walls of protective armor.

The Roman Empire stretched from Scotland to Syria at its height in the second century A.D. It later split into two kingdoms, the east and the west. In the fifth and sixth centuries A.D., the original western empire fell to the onslaught of tribes from the north—the Huns, Goths, and Vandals. Nonetheless, Roman civilization—with its laws, arts, literature, roads, and aqueducts—influenced the development of Europe for centuries to come.

SAMURAI

merging in the feudal society of 12th-century Japan, the Samurai were a military class—knights, so to speak—divided into various clans led by Shoguns. At the height of their influence, they formed much of the ruling class of Japan.

Samurai warriors wore a highly ornate, functional armor, accompanied by horrific masks to instill fear in their opponents. They are probably best known for their swords, which bore the same name. Curved to facilitate broad, slashing cuts rather than stabbing thrusts, the blades displayed some of the finest military craftsmanship in the history of the world. Samurai steel was reworked as many as 20 times and sometimes combined with iron before it was hammered and tempered by fire to give the blades incredible strength and razor sharpness.

In battle, Samurai might carry as many as five swords of varying lengths—one reserved for the warrior's suicide in the event of disgrace in battle, a practice called *hara-kiri*. But the Samurai sword also held both social and spiritual significance. When highly adorned, it displayed the social rank and character of the person wearing it. Unsheathed, it represented the warrior's very soul.

Similar to the rigid codes of chivalry knights of medieval Europe were expected to follow both on the field of battle and off, the Samurai adhered to a noble code of ethics called *bushido*, "the way of the warrior."

The Samurai were proud and often illiterate, but many were well schooled and considered themselves poets as well as warriors. Still, as fighting men they accepted a life of Spartan discipline. Japan's feudal system collapsed in the second half of the 19th century.

SAXONS

Like the Angles and Jutes, the Saxons were a Teutonic people originating on the Jutland peninsula—present-day Denmark. According to Ptolemy, a Greek mathematician and geographer, they inhabited the Jutland province of Schleswig in the second century A.D.

Toward the close of the third century and continuing into the fourth, the Saxons were known as seafaring pirates in the North Sea who beat travelers into submission and plundered their possessions.

Starting in the second half of the fourth century, they invaded provinces held by the still-powerful Roman Empire. During the fifth and sixth centuries, after Roman power had fallen, Saxons captured lands in northwest Germany, the northern coast of France, and southeast England. Aided by the Angles and the Jutes, they pushed the native Celts of Britain from their home territories, into Wales and Scotland, and settled in their place.

In Germany and northern France, the Saxons battled the Franks during the eighth century. The Franks often held the upper hand under the leadership of King Pepin the Short, son of Charles Martel, who had earlier defeated the Muslim forces invading southern France. Martel's grandson, Charlemagne, continued to raid Saxon lands in Germany and France until the pagan Saxons were finally subdued in 804 and converted to Christianity.

The Saxons in Britain melded with the Angles and the Jutes to become the Anglo-Saxons, who held sway in England until subdued by the invading Norman King William the Conqueror in 1066. The Saxons in Germany and France remained under Frankish rule until they ultimately vanished from the region.

TARTARS

The collective peoples known as the Tartars evolved from the Mongols, a race of fierce, nomadic horsemen from the steppes of central Asia. The combination of their barbarity in battle with clever, fearless military leaders made them the masters of nearly three quarters of the known world in their heyday.

Also known as Tatars, the Tartars merged with other Mongol clans following the fabled conquests of the Mongol leader Genghis Khan in the 13th century. Their army was as disciplined as it was savage—perhaps as disciplined as the legions of Rome centuries earlier. Equipped with powerful bows, Mongol archers on horseback were said to have been able to hit moving targets from distances of 1,000 feet.

Mongol groups ruled much of modern-day Russia in the 13th and 14th centuries, forming less of an empire than a group of vassal states. The overall Mongol dominance extended from China in the east, across central Asia to Persia and Asia Minor in the west. To the north, the conquering realm of the Tartars reached to Poland and Hungary. To the south, Mongols ruled northern India.

Over the following centuries, their power began to wane and they saw the gradual disintegration and division of their once proud but savage empire. By the 15th century, the Tartars had become much like the people they were when they started out—nomadic tribesmen of central Asia. The last Tartar stronghold, Crimea, was annexed to Russia in 1783, though they now control a distinct republic within Russia.

A Muslim people, Tartars live today as an ethnic group, rather than as a military force. Most reside in eastern European Russia and the Ural Mountains.

TROJANS

The Trojans were probably a civilized, cultured, and noble race, but their history is clouded by myth and legend. Troy was the prominent city in the *Iliad,* an epic work by the Greek poet Homer. In his version, the Trojan War, a decade-long siege, was fought over the beautiful Helen, wife of the Spartan king Menelaus. Her heart—along with the rest of her—was stolen by the Trojan prince Paris.

Menelaus's brother, King Agamemnon, led an army, which included the legendary warrior Achilles, to avenge the insult to Menelaus. The two sides fought furiously, often in hand-to-hand combat, using spears, javelins, and horse-drawn chariots. After 10 years, the Greeks took Troy using a diabolical contraption known as "the Trojan Horse." With Greeks hiding inside it, the horse was welcomed into the city. At nightfall the Greeks emerged to sack and burn Troy.

The historical city of Troy is thought to have been unearthed in 1870 in a mound called Hissarlik on the Dardanelles in present-day Turkey. The mound includes at least nine cities built one atop another over the ages.

In Homer's version, Troy was destroyed by fire. Evidence from the modern excavations indicates that the ruins include a city burned in the early 12th century B.C.—the era traditionally given for the Trojan War. Historians believe the actual causes of the war were probably the more common ones, namely conquest and greed.

In myth, the Trojan War resulted in the city's destruction. In history, the Trojans fought frequently with the Greeks, and many Trojan cities were sacked. The warriors of Troy, however, were noted for their courage and endurance, hence the expression: "He bore the pain like a Trojan."

VANDALS

The word "vandalism" is derived from the name of this Germanic warrior tribe, who called themselves Wandals, or "wanderers." The Vandals, of Teutonic stock, were famous for their savagery in battle and their destruction of cities, as the modern term indicates.

They originated in an area stretching from the shores of the Baltic Sea to the middle region of the Danube River, centered in the eastern part of modern Hungary. To escape the Huns invading from the east, they poured westward into Gaul (now France) in A.D. 406. In 409 they invaded Spain, fighting against—and losing to—the Visigoths, who were then fighting in the service of Rome.

The Vandals left Spain in 429 under their new ruler, Gaiseric, to invade North Africa but were defeated by the Romans a year later. The Roman victory was short-lived, however, and the Vandals rose again to rule North Africa for 100 years.

They dominated the area of modern Algeria and northern Morocco by roughly 435, then took Carthage, their major victory, in 439. The Vandals' pirate fleets spread terror throughout the Mediterranean Sea, dominating its western segment. In 455, they joined with several other "barbarian" tribes to invade and sack Rome—earning them the reputation of "destroyers of civilization."

Gaiseric's death in 477 marked the start of the Vandals' decline. In 533, the Byzantine emperor Justinian sent his general, Belisarius, to North Africa to tame them, and the Vandals were fully vanquished, putting an end to the looting and plundering of these proud, seafaring rovers.

VIKINGS

The most notorious sea rovers of all time emerged from the deep inlets of the Scandinavian coasts. The Vikings, a conglomerate of Nordic peoples—Danes, Norwegians, and Swedes—established the Viking Age in the 9th through 11th centuries A.D. Relative late-comers to world conquest, they still left an indelible mark.

The origin of the name "Viking" remains in dispute. Some claim it comes from the Old Norse noun *vik,* meaning "inlet," or the verb *vika,* meaning "to go off." Others maintain that it derives from the Old English word *wic,*—a camp or fortified trade settlement.

The latter fits with the notion that Vikings were as much roving traders as pirates and pillagers. Either way, they were valiant warriors who navigated the seas in long, black galleys powered by oars and colorful, intimidating sails. The sight of their "dragon ships" breaking the horizon is said to have sent shivers down the spines of opponents. A pagan race, the Vikings were antagonistic toward the ever-spreading Christian faith and seemed to delight in slaughtering the inhabitants of the territories they conquered.

The Vikings braved the frigid northern seas to visit Greenland, and their expeditions are believed to have reached North America, though historians were slow to accept this idea, because the rest of Europe knew nothing of such trips. In the ninth century, the Vikings crossed Russia by way of lakes and rivers, all the way to the Mediterranean Sea.

Eventually, the Vikings became Christians, and their random raids became invasions that led them to conquer and settle the Normandy coast of France and parts of England.

CHRONOLOGY

922 B.C.	After King Solomon's death, the Israelite kingdom divides into Israel and Judah.
814 B.C.	Ancient Carthage in North Africa established by Phoenicians.
745 B.C.	Assyrians conquer Babylonians.
753 B.C.	City of Rome is founded.
612 B.C.	Nineveh falls to Babylonians, ending Assyrian civilization.
558–559 B.C.	Persians win freedom from Medes under Cyrus the Great and defeat Babylonians.
330 B.C.	Alexander the Great starts 10-year expansion of Macedonian (Greek) empire.
264–241 B.C.	First Punic War; Romans defeat Carthaginians.
218–202 B.C.	Second Punic War, ending in Carthaginian general Hannibal's crushing defeat; Carthage sues for peace.
149–146 B.C.	Third Punic War; Romans devastate Carthage.
A.D. 247	Goths begin raids on Roman Empire.
250	Franks wander into Roman provinces.
395	Visigoths renounce allegiance to Rome and invade Greece and Italy.
410	Visigoths sack Rome under King Alaric and invade Spain and southern Gaul.
428	Vandals leave Spain for North Africa under Gaiseric; eventually taking Algeria, Morocco, and Carthage.

450   Angles, Saxons, and Jutes invade England.

451   Huns invade Gaul.

453   Death of Attila; Huns' power declines.

455   Vandals and other tribes sack Rome.

493   Theodoric becomes first Gothic ruler of western
       Roman Empire.

533   Byzantine General Belisarius tames Vandals.

800   Scandinavians begin the Viking Age.

1066   William the Conqueror of Normandy wrests
       English throne from King Harold II.

1251   Mongol warriors led by Kublai Khan conquer
       China.

1368   Revolt under Ming Dynasty restores China's
       independence.

1453   Ottoman Turks take Byzantine capital of Con-
       stantinople and later conquer Syria, Egypt, and
       Arabia.

1519   Spaniard Hernando Cortez invades Aztecs.

1530   Spaniard Francisco Pizarro invades and conquers
       Inca Empire in Peru.

1870   Stone walls and battlements believed to have
       been the city of Troy unearthed in modern-day
       Turkey.

1918   World War I ends; Ottoman Empire dissolves.

INDEX ❀

FURTHER READING

Boyle, Charles (senior editor). *Time Frame: The Enterprise of War.* Alexandria, Va.: Time-Life Books, 1991.

Grun, Bernard. *The Timetables of History.* New York: Simon & Schuster, 1991.

Jones, Gwyn. *A History of the Vikings.* Oxford: Oxford University Press, 1984.

Jones, Prudence, and Nigel Pennick. *A History of Pagan Europe.* New York: Routledge, 1995.

Keegan, John. *A History of Warfare.* New York: Alfred A. Knopf, 1993.

Newark, Tim. *Celtic Warriors.* London: Blanford Press, 1994.